Alexa skills for Kids and Teens – Fun Skills for Amazon Echo Devices

By Stu Armstrong

ISBN: **978-1983804984**

ISBN13: **1983804983**

Copyright Stu Armstrong 2018 ©

All rights reserved

This book may not be reproduced in way shape or form, the work is reserved to the copyright holder S Armstrong 2018 ©

www.stuarmstrong.com

Contents

FUN SOUNDS	8
4AFART	9
Meow!	9
Sleep and Relaxation Sunds	9
4ABURP	9
Burp me	10
Ocean Sounds	10
Fake Laugh	10
Jurrasic Bark	10
Thunderstorm Sounds	11
Rain Sounds	11
Rain Forrest	11
Ambiant Sounds	11
Beautiful dream	12

Fireplace Sounds	12
Doctor Who	12
Laugh Box	12
Boo	13
Applause	13
FUN AND GAMES	**14**
Animal Game	15
Akinator	15
Ditty	15
Question of the Day	15
Would you rather	16
True or False	16
Magic Door	16
Open Your Mind	16
Beautiful dream	17
Deal or No Deal	17
Yes Sire!	17
Destiny	17
Trivial Poursuit	18

Millionare Quiz game	18
Beat the Into	18
Monte	19
Little Light Destiny Two	19
True or False	19
Jepody	20
Who wants to be a millionare	20
20 Questions	20
Tic-Tac-Toe	20
Would You Rather	21
Hangman	21
Superheroes	21
Bingo	21

EDUCATIONAL — 22

Spelling Bee	23
Math Mania	23
1-2-3 Math	23
Curiosity	23
Dinosaur Facts	24

Dog Facts	24
Cat Facts	24
Guess the Number	24
Capital Quiz	25
The Name Game	25
English Translator	25

STORIES   26

Magic Door	27
Bedtime Story	27
Beautiful dream	27
Short Bedtime Story	28
Earplay	28

JOKES   29

Tell me a Joke	30
Dirty Joke (Child freindly)	30
Knock Knock Jokes	30
Yo Mamma Jokes	30

OTHER ACTIVITIES   31

Inspire me	**32**
Nintendo Switch	**32**
Christmas Kindness	**32**
CompliBot	**32**
PokeyFinder	**33**
Sheep Count	**33**
Sesame Street	**33**

Fun Sounds

4AFART

Alexa, Ask for a Fart

Meow!

Alexa, Meow Meow

Sleep and Relaxation Sunds

Alexa, Open Sleep sounds

4ABURP

Alexa, Ask for a Burp

Burp me

Alexa, Open Burp Me

Ocean Sounds

Alexa, Open Ocean Sounds

Fake Laugh

Aleza, Open Fake Laugh

Jurrasic Bark

Alexa, Open Jurrasic Bark

Thunderstorm Sounds

Alea, Play thunderstporm sounds

Rain Sounds

Alea, Play rain sounds

Rain Forrest

Alexa, Play Rain Forrest sounds

Ambiant Sounds

Alexa, Play Ambiemnbt

Beautiful dream

Alex, Open Beautiful Dream

Fireplace Sounds

Alexa, Play Fireplace sounds

Doctor Who

Alexa, as the Tardis box to land

Laugh Box

Alexa, Ask Laugh Box for a Baby Laugh

Boo

Alexa, Ask Boo

Applause

Alexa, Ask Applause

Fun and Games

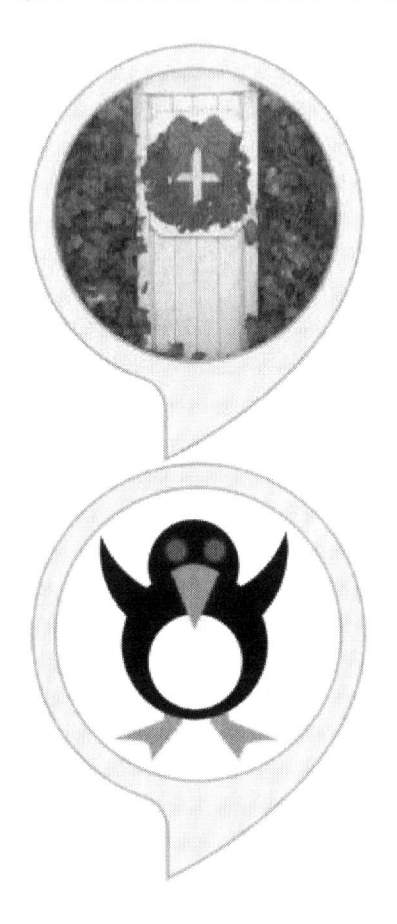

Animal Game

Alexa, Start Animal Game

Akinator

Alexa, Start Akinator

Ditty

Alexa, Open Ditty

Question of the Day

Alexa, Open question of the day

Would you rather

Alexa, Would you rather

True or False

Alexa, Plkay true or false

Magic Door

Alexa, Open Magic Door

Open Your Mind

Alexa, Open your mind

Beautiful dream

Alex, Open Beautiful Dream

Deal or No Deal

Alexa, Play Deal or no Deal

Yes Sire!

Alexa, Play Yes Sire

Destiny

Alexa, Ask ghost to tell me my next milestone

Alexa, Ask ghoist to tell me my best weapen

Trivial Poursuit

Alexa, Open Trival Pursuit

Alexa, Play Trival Pursuity

Millionare Quiz game

Alexa, Open Millioaire quiz game

Beat the Into

Alexa, Play beat the intro

Monte

Alexa, Ask launch button Monte

Little Light Destiny Two

Alexa, Little Light Destiny 2

True or False

Alexa, Open True or False

Alxea, Play True or False

Jepody

Alexa, Open Jepody

Who wants to be a millionare

Alexa, Open Millionare quiz game

20 Questions

Alexa, Play 20 questions

Tic-Tac-Toe

Alexa, Ask Tic Tac Toe for a Game

Would You Rather

Alexa, Play Would You Rather

Hangman

Alexa, Ask Hangman for a Game

Superheroes

Alexa, Ask Super Heroes Who Spiderman Is

Bingo

Alexa, Open Bingo

Educational

Interpreter

Spelling Bee

Alexa, Launch Spelling Bee

Math Mania

Alexa, Ask Math Mania to Play

1-2-3 Math

ALEXA, OPEN 1-2-3

Curiosity

Alexa, Open Curiosity

Dinosaur Facts

Alexa, Open Dinosaur Facts

Dog Facts

Alexa, Open Dog Facts

Cat Facts

Alexa, Open Cat Facts

Guess the Number

Alexa, Launch Guess the Number

Capital Quiz

Alexa, Tell Capital Quiz to Start Practicing

The Name Game

Alexa, Open the Name Game and Use Alexa

English Translator

Alexa, Open English Translator

Stories

Magic Door

Alexa, Open Magic Door

Bedtime Story

Alexa, Tell Bedtime story to ....(Your name)

Beautiful dream

Alex, Open Beautiful Dream

Short Bedtime Story

Alexa, Open Bed Time Story

Earplay

Alexa, Start Earplay

Jokes

YO MAMA JOKES

Tell me a Joke

Alexa, Tell me a Joke

Dirty Joke (Child freindly)

Alexa, Tell me a dirty joke

Knock Knock Jokes

Alexa, Open Knock Knock

Yo Mamma Jokes

Alexa, Tell me a Yo Momma Joke

Other Activities

Inspire me

Aalexa, Insipire me

Nintendo Switch

Alexa, Open Nintendo Switch unoiffical lates releases

Christmas Kindness

Alexa, Ask Christmas Kindness for an Idea

CompliBot

Alexa, Open CompliBot

PokeyFinder

Alexa, Ask Pokey Finder to Find Pikachu

Sheep Count

Alexa, Start Sheep Count

Sesame Street

Alexa, Open Sesame Street

ISBN: **978-1983804984**

ISBN13: **1983804983**

Copyright Stu Armstrong 2018 ©

All rights reserved

This book may not be reproduced in way shape or form, the work is reserved to the copyright holder S Armstrong 2018 ©

www.stuarmstrong.com

Printed in Great Britain
by Amazon